AUSTRALIAN WILDLIFE

Mason Crest Publishers
www.masoncrest.com
Philadelphia

Mason Crest Publishers
370 Reed Road
Broomall, PA 19008
(866) MCP-BOOK (toll free)

First printing

ISBN 1-59084-210-3

Library of Congress Cataloging-in-Publication Data on file at the Library of Congress

First published by Steve Parish Publishing Pty Ltd
PO Box 1058, Archerfield BC
Queensland 4108, Australia
© Copyright Steve Parish Publishing Pty Ltd

Photography by Steve Parish, with
    Stanley Breeden: pp. 12 (Northern Quoll), 18, 24, 26 (Diadem Horseshoe & insect-eating bats), 27, 34, 36, 40-41
    (Woma Python), 44, 44-45, 46-47, 48 (Leafwing Butterfly), 49; Jiri Lochman: pp. 12 (Western Quolls), 16; M & I Morcombe:
    pp. 12 (Kultarr), 16-17, 25; Belinda Wright: pp. 20, 39, 42-43, 21 (Cairns Birdwing Butterfly); Museum of Queensland: p. 21;
    Graeme Chapman: pp. 36-37; Ian Morris: pp. 43 (top), 46

Printed in Jordan

Writing, editing, design, and production by Steve Parish Publishing Pty Ltd, Australia

CONTENTS

▽

Use of Capital Letters for Animal Names in this book
An animal's official common name begins with a capital letter.
Otherwise the name begins with a lowercase letter.

AUSTRALIAN WILDLIFE

Nearly everyone has heard of the kangaroo and the koala, but there are many other interesting animals that live in Australia as well.

Some animals are strange and fascinating, like the Platypus and the Echidna. Others are furry and shy, like wombats and bandicoots. There are colorful parrots and noisy kookaburras in the trees, sea lions in the seas, and crocodiles in the wetlands.

Australian wildlife is full of surprises and wonders to enjoy.

◄ Kookaburra

Common Wombat and friends. ▲

KANGAROOS

A kangaroo is a marsupial. Its young develops in a pouch. There are many different sorts of kangaroos. All have strong hind legs and long feet. A kangaroo does not walk—it hops. Its long and heavy tail balances the front part of its body as it jumps along. If a kangaroo is startled, it can hop as fast as a moving car.

▲ Pretty-Face Wallaby and joey.

▲ Red Kangaroo   Grey Kangaroo ▶

KOALAS

Koalas spend most of their time sleeping. For a few hours each day they eat gum leaves. This food does not give Koalas much energy, so they have to eat a lot to be able to keep warm and move around.

A mother Koala carries her baby in her pouch until it is big enough to ride on her back. It puts its nose into her pouch to drink. A Koala may stay with its mother for two years before leaving to find its own home.

Mother Koala with young one. ▲ ▶

WOMBATS

A wombat is also a marsupial. The tiny newborn grows in its mother's pouch. The female wombat's pouch faces backwards so that when she digs a burrow, the dirt does not get inside it. The burrow is a place for sleeping and hiding from enemies. Wombats have strong front legs and claws for digging. They feed at night on grass and leaves.

There are plenty of Common Wombats in Australia, but Hairy-Nosed Wombats are very rare.

◄ ▲ Common Wombat

Northern Hairy-Nosed Wombat ▲

MARSUPIAL CARNIVORES

▲ Northern Quoll   Kultarr ▼

▲ Baby Western Quolls   Tasmanian Devil ▶

Many of Australia's marsupials are carnivores. Carnivores eat other animals. The largest marsupial carnivore is the Tasmanian Devil. It likes to eat animals that are already dead.

Quolls are also carnivores. They eat smaller animals, such as birds, mice, and insects. The Kultarr is a small carnivore that lives in the desert. Kultarrs eat centipedes, scorpions, and lizards.

▲ Bilby

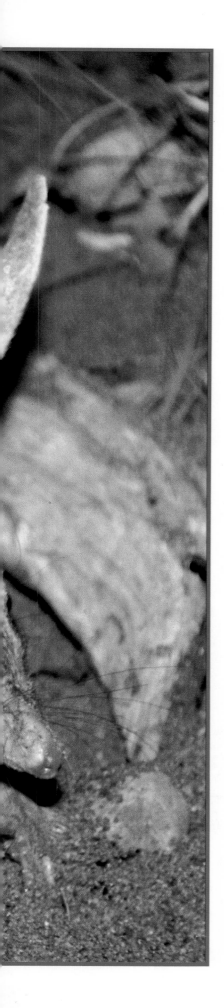

BANDICOOTS

Bandicoots are marsupials that live on the ground and use their front paws to dig up burrowing spiders, insects, and underground fungus to eat.

The Bilby is a rare bandicoot with soft fur and long ears. It lives in the Australian desert and shelters in a burrow during the heat of the day. It comes out to feed at night.

Western Barred Bandicoot ▲

NUMBATS

A Numbat is a marsupial with gold-and-brown fur, stripes on its back and face, and a long and bushy tail. Unlike many marsupials, Numbats are active during the day.

Numbats eat termites. A Numbat opens the trails leading from termite nests with its paws and licks up insects with its long, sticky tongue.

Numbats only live in a small area of forest in Western Australia. They are very rare and are threatened by foxes and bushfires.

▲ Young Numbats

Adult Numbat ▶

POSSUMS

Possums live in trees. They have sharp claws to hold on tight. Ringtail possums can also hang from their curling tails. Possums come out at night to feed on leaves, sap, and fruit. Some possums eat insects.

Possums are marsupials, too. A newborn baby possum lives in its mother's pouch, feeding on her milk for four to five months. Then the young possum rides on its mother's back until it is big enough to find its own food.

▲ Herbert River Ringtail Possum

Female Common Brushtail Possum and baby. ▶

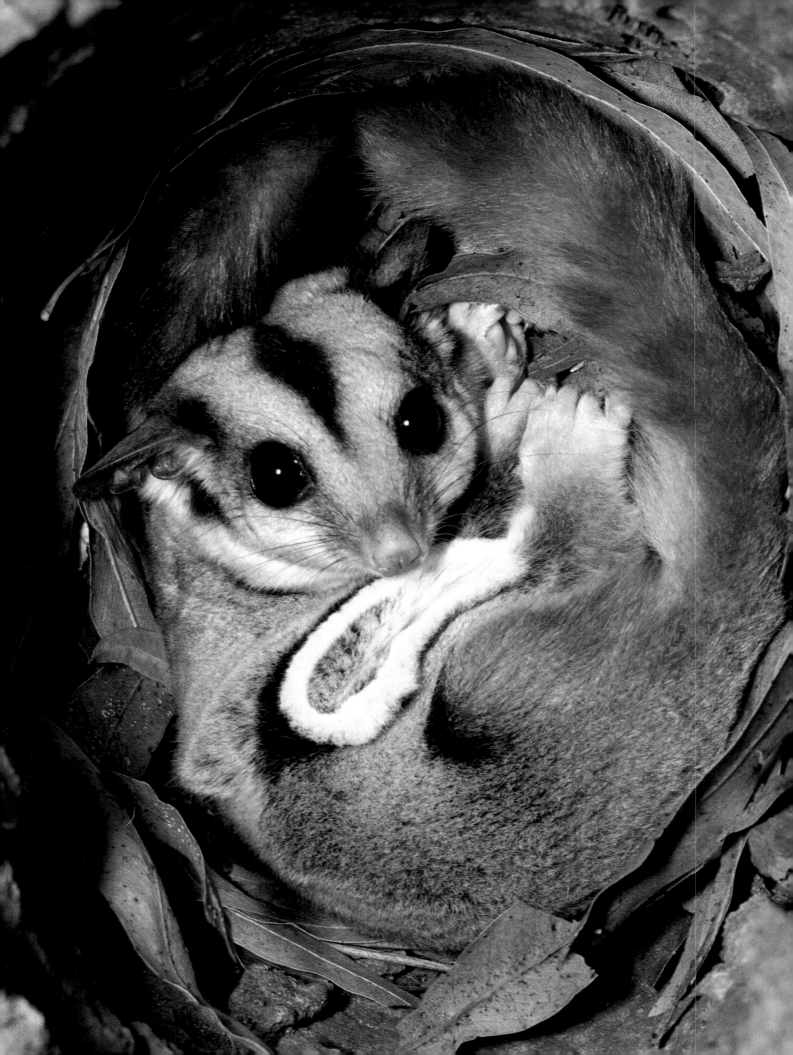

GLIDERS

Gliders are marsupials that have flaps of skin joining their front and hind legs. They can glide through the air from tree to tree in the forest.

The largest glider is the Greater Glider. Gliders and possums are similar, but possums have no flaps of skin to glide through the trees.

Greater Glider ▲

◄ Sugar Glider in its nest.

Mahogany Glider ▲

PLATYPUS

The Platypus catches its food in creeks and rivers. It has thick, waterproof fur that keeps it warm in the cool water. When a Platypus dives, it closes its eyes, ears, and nostrils, but its bill can feel the tiny electric signals given out by small water animals, like worms. The Platypus grabs the animals in its bill, stores them in its cheek pouches, and then returns to the surface of the water to eat them.

▲ Platypus

ECHiDNAS

The Short-Beaked Echidna is covered with long spines. It has strong claws for digging. The echidna digs into an ant or termite nest and pokes in its long, sticky tongue. Then the echidna pulls out its tongue and swallows the insects on it.

When an echidna sees an enemy, it digs into the ground to hide. If the ground is hard, the echidna rolls up into a spiky ball.

Short-Beaked Echidna ▲

23

RODENTS

A rodent's sharp front teeth keep growing all its life. They have to be kept worn down by gnawing on things.

Although there were harmful rats and mice brought to Australia by settlers, there are many native Australian rodents.

Some are very rare and are hunted by animals such as wild cats and foxes.

Some rodents live in burrows or hollow trees, but others make nests. The desert hopping-mice feed at night on seeds and can survive with little water.

▲ Brush-Tailed Rabbit-Rats

Spinifex Hopping-Mouse ▶

BATS

Bats are the only mammals that can fly. A bat's long fingers are joined by thin skin to make wings.

To find insects to eat, small bats send out shrill noises. The bats can then hear the sounds that bounce off flying insects. This is called echolocation.

Big bats that eat fruit and flowers do not use echolocation. They find food by smell, by sight, and by following noises made by other feeding bats.

Diadem Horseshoe Bat ▲

▲ Insect-eating bat

Spectacled Flying Fox ▲

Queensland Blossom Bat ▲

DINGOES

Dingoes are dogs. The first Dingoes to reach Australia came across the sea with people from Asia. Some became wild, and Dingoes now live in many habitats across Australia. Most have sand-colored coats, but some are black or cream in color.

They have keen senses of sight, smell, and hearing for hunting. A Dingo living alone catches small animals to eat, but a family group will catch large animals, such as kangaroos.

A desert Dingo ▲

◀ A Dingo pants to cool itself.

A Dingo hunting along a beach. ▲

SEA LiONS

Australian Sea Lions live in two different sorts of habitat. They spend most of the year in the sea, then leave the water once a year to breed on beaches on Australia's southern coast.

On these beaches, each female sea lion gives birth to a pup. The pup feeds on its mother's milk until it has learned to swim and catch fish to eat.

Sea lions hunt in cold sea water. Their fur and a thick layer of fat under the skin keeps them warm. Their feet and hands have become flippers. They are fast and graceful swimmers.

Australian Sea Lions ▲ ▶

PARROTS

▲ Male Australian King Parrot

Crimson Rosella ▲

A parrot is a bird with a curved beak and bright feathers. Two of its toes point forwards and two point backwards. A parrot sometimes holds its food in one foot while eating. Parrots eat seeds and fruit.

A cockatoo is a big parrot with long feathers on its head. When the cockatoo is excited, the feathers stand up in a crest. Cockatoos fly in noisy flocks and usually nest in tree hollows, where they lay their eggs.

Sulphur-Crested Cockatoo ▶

WATERBiRDS

Some waterbirds are good swimmers. Black Swan cygnets swim soon after they hatch, then follow their parents across the water.

Some waterbirds are good waders. The Jabiru wades through shallow water on its long, red legs, catching fish, frogs, and snakes with its long beak.

The Comb-Crested Jacana looks as if it is walking on the water as it runs across the lily leaves.

Jabiru wading. ▲

◄ Comb-Crested Jacana and its eggs.

Black Swan and cygnets. ▲

FLYING FEATHERS

A bird's body is covered by feathers. Soft, fluffy feathers keep the bird warm and dry, and the long feathers on its wings and tail help it to fly. When the Spectacled Monarch sits on its nest, the grey feathers on its back help it hide from its enemies. Male and female birds of the same kind sometimes have feathers of different colors and shapes.

▲ Spectacled Monarch

Female and male Purple-Crowned Fairy-Wrens ▲

BiRDS OF PREY

Birds of prey are hunters, with strong legs and feet and sharp claws. Their hooked beaks tear up the animals they eat.

The White-Bellied Sea Eagle catches fish, but may also eat dead fish or other animals that have washed up on the beach.

The Wedge-Tailed Eagle flies at great heights and has keen eyesight. It swoops down to grab prey it can see on the ground.

◄ Wedge-Tailed Eagle

Adult White-Bellied Sea Eagle and chick. ▲

REPTILES

Snakes, lizards, turtles, and crocodiles are reptiles. Their skins are dry, not slimy, and covered with scales or bony plates. Reptiles do not make their own body heat. In cold weather, a reptile must lie in the sun to warm its body. It needs body heat to be able to move quickly, find food, and escape enemies.

▲ Central Netted Ground Dragon

▲ Thorny Devil

Woma Python ▼

SALTWATER
CROCODILES

▲ Saltwater Crocodile

The Saltwater (or Estuarine) Crocodile lives in salty coastal creeks and in fresh water in Northern Australia. A Saltwater Crocodile has strong jaws and sharp teeth. Its eyes and nostrils are on the top of its head and snout. Its skin is covered with strong scales, like armor.

A crocodile catches fish and other animals in the water. It can grab a big animal from the riverbank and drag it under the water to eat.

◄ ▲ Saltwater Crocodile

FRiLLED LiZARDS

When a Frilled Lizard is scared, it spreads its neck frill wide, opens its mouth, and hisses. It looks fierce, but it is not really dangerous. If raising its frill and hissing does not frighten an enemy, this lizard will not stay and fight.

To get away from danger, the lizard rises on its hind legs and runs. It may climb a tree and then stay on the other side of the trunk from its enemy. Frilled Lizards eat insects and other small animals.

▲ Frilled Lizard running.   Frilled Lizard facing an enemy. ▶

FROGS

Frogs are amphibians—animals that live in both the water and on land. Frogs have soft, moist skins and need to stay in damp places so they do not dry out. A tree frog's fingers and toes end in round pads, which help it climb surfaces as smooth as glass.

▲ Corroboree Frog

▲ Day's Frog   White-Lipped Tree Frog ▶

BUTTERFLIES

▼ Leafwing Butterfly

Cairns Birdwing Butterfly ▲

Butterflies and moths hatch from eggs as caterpillars. A caterpillar makes a cocoon. In the cocoon, it goes into a resting stage, called a pupa. The pupa changes into an adult. Then the moth or butterfly comes out, stretches its wings, and flies away.

AND MOTHS

Zodiac Moth ▲

INDEX OF ANIMALS PICTURED

FURTHER READING & INTERNET RESOURCES

For more information on Australia's animals, check out the following books and Web sites.

Arnold, Caroline. Australian Animals. (August 2000) HarperCollins Juvenile Books; ISBN: 0688167667

Seventeen unusual animals from Australia are introduced in this full-color book, including koalas, possums, gliders, quolls, Tasmanian devils, platypuses, echidnas, kangaroos, wombats, dingoes, snakes, and penguins.

Langeland, Deidre, Frank Ordaz (illustrator), and Ranye Kaye (narrator). (April 1998) Soundprints Corp. Audio; ISBN: 156899544X

Kangaroo Island: The Story of an Australian Mallee Forest. As morning comes to Kangaroo Island following a thunderstorm, a mother kangaroo finds her lost baby, and a burned eucalyptus tree sprouts buds and becomes a new home for animals. The cassette that comes with the book adds sounds of sea lions barking, sea gulls calling, crickets humming, and even a raging forest fire.

Morpurgo, Michael, Christian Birmingham (illustrator). *Wombat Goes Walkabout.* (April 2000) Candlewick Press; ISBN: 0763611689

As Wombat wanders through the Australian bush in search of his mother, he encounters a variety of creatures demanding to know who he is and what he can do.

Paul, Tessa. *Down Under (Animal Trackers Around the World).* (May 1998) Crabtree Publishers; ISBN: 0865055963

The book features beautiful illustrations of each animal, its tracks, diet, and environment and includes interesting facts about how each animal lives. Australian animals featured include the platypus, the dingo, the kiwi, the kangaroo, the emu, the koala, the kookaburra, and the Tasmanian devil.

http://home.mira.net/~areadman/aussie.htm

This fabulous Web site is dedicated to the creatures of Australia. It contains a comprehensive listing of the animals of Australia, each of which is a link to more in-depth information about Australia's wildlife.

http://www.australianwildlife.com.au/

This Web site is just one in a ring of sites dedicated to wildlife. Visitors can find cool desktop themes, interesting news articles, book reviews, and more—all pertaining to the wildlife of Australia.

http://www.onthenet.com.au/~jbergh/koala /Welcome.html

This site is perfect for students of any age wishing to learn more about the koala—one of Australia's more unique creatures. In this site, visitors will find questions from students of various ages and the answers, facts about koalas (versus myths), pictures of koalas, information on their anatomy, and more.

http://ausinternet.com/ettamogah/siteindex.htm

This is the Web site for the Ettamogah Wildlife Sanctuary. Visitors to the site will find information on the various types of Australian wildlife there and can take "virtual" guided tours of the park. There is even a special activities page for kids.

http://users.orac.net.au/~mhumphry/ austwild.html

This Web site has information on a few of the more "famous" members of Australia's wildlife. Read interesting facts about kangaroos, koalas, wombats, kookaburras, emus, platypuses, and echidnas.

NATURE KIDS SERIES

Birdlife
Australia is home to some of the most interesting, colorful, and noisy birds on earth. Discover some of the many different types, including parrots, kingfishers, and owls.

Frogs and Reptiles
Australia has a wide variety of environments, and there is at least one frog or reptile that calls each environment home. Discover the frogs and reptiles living in Australia.

Kangaroos and Wallabies
The kangaroo is one of the most well-known Australian creatures. Learn interesting facts about kangaroos and wallabies, a close cousin.

Marine Fish
The ocean surrounding Australia is home to all sorts of marine fish. Discover their interesting shapes, sizes, and colors, and learn about the different types of habitat in the ocean.

Rainforest Animals
Australia's rainforests are home to a wide range of animals, including snakes, birds, frogs, and wallabies. Discover a few of the creatures that call the rainforests home.

Rare & Endangered Wildlife
Animals all over the world need our help to keep from becoming extinct. Learn about the special creatures in Australia that are in danger of disappearing forever.

Sealife
Australia is surrounded by sea. As a result, there is an amazing variety of life that lives in these waters. Dolphins, crabs, reef fish, and eels are just a few of the animals highlighted in this book.

Wildlife
Australia is known for its unique creatures, such as the kangaroo and the koala. Read about these and other special creatures that call Australia home.